Series concept and design: Liz Black
Book design: Jane Hawkins
Commissioning Editor: Lisa Edwards
Editor: Katie Orchard
Science Consultant: Dr Carol Ballard

Published in Great Britain in 2002 as Which Switch is Which?
by Hodder Wayland, an imprint of Hodder Children's Books

This paperback edition published in 2009 by Wayland,
an imprint of Hachette Children's Books,
338 Euston Road, London NW1 3BH
www.hachettelivre.co.uk

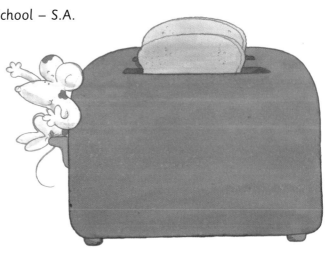

Cataloguing in publication data
Godwin, Sam
Switch on, Switch off: A first look at electricity (Little Bees)
1. Electricity - Juvenile literature
I. Title
537

ISBN 978 07502 5877 7

Printed and bound in China

Switch on, Switch off

A first look at electricity

Switch on, Switch off
A first look at electricity

Sam Godwin

WAYLAND

It is night-time. All is quiet and still.

Come on, let's find something to eat.

7

9

So we turn on the lights.

11

Electricity comes from a power station.

It flows along wires and into our homes.

So, the wires must come in through a hole in the wall!

Other wires carry the electricity around the home,

14

to switches in every room.

That's neat and tidy!

from the switches to the lights.

17

Electricity not only gives us light.

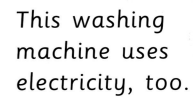

26

29

All about electricity

When it's dark, we need electric light to be able to see clearly.

Electricity travels into our homes along wires. The wires are connected to switches around the home.

Pressing a switch turns a light on.

Pressing a switch turns a light off.

Electricity makes lots of things work around the home.

It can make things hot or cold.

It can make sound.

And it can make things move.

Useful Words

Plug
This connects electrical objects to switches.

Power station
A place where electricity is made.

Shock
Electricity can pass through people and give them a nasty shock.

Switch
This can turn on or off the supply of electricity to an object.

Important
Electricity can be dangerous:

• Always ask an adult to turn on switches for you.

• Never touch any switches or plugs with wet hands.

• Never play with electric objects.